MODERN-DAY
MIRACLES

DUANE McKEY

Editor: Nancy Costa

Copy editor: Michele Stotz

Designer: Mark Bond

©Copyright 2025 Adventist World Radio.
All rights reserved. Used by permission.

Adventist World Radio is an official media ministry of the
General Conference of Seventh-day Adventists
12501 Old Columbia Pike
Silver Spring, MD 20904, United States

Printed in the U.S.A. by Remnant Publications, Coldwater, Michigan
ISBN: 979-8-9988929-0-5

For additional copies, please visit:
awr.org/miracles

TABLE OF CONTENTS

Foreword: Seven Pieces of Spaghetti 5
1. Miracle in the Congo 10
2. Stopped at the Border! 13
3. The Missing Tickets 20
4. A Modern-Day Witch 22
5. The Fortune Teller's Story 24
6. My Mother's Prayer 26
7. The Witch Cow Thief 27
8. The Can Opener That Didn't Work 29
9. The AWR Chickens 31
10. Four Gallons of Glue 33
11. Mohammed and the Imam 35
12. "Alexa" Shares the Truth 39
13. In a Hurry to Die! 41
14. Miracle in Malibu 43
15. Anil and His Atheist Friend 44
16. The Unexpected Evangelist 46
17. The Unusual Visitor 48
18. The Encounter at Taita Falcon Lodge 51
19. Barbie's Incredible Story 56
20. Machiel Van Wyk, the Afrikaner Farmer 59
21. The Miracle of the Tithing Cows 63
22. Young-Woong's Testimony 67
23. Miracle in Ukraine 69
24. The Blueberry Farmer and the Methodist Church 73
25. The 51-Year Dream 76

FOREWORD

SEVEN PIECES OF SPAGHETTI
The Calling That Changed Everything

WHILE IN MY THIRD YEAR AS A THEOLOGY MAJOR at Union College in Lincoln, Nebraska, I worked in construction putting up Butler steel buildings. I enjoyed the hard work, hanging 20 feet off the ground with my legs wrapped around steel frames often covered with ice, erecting the building frames. This was a man's job, and I was proud of it. But my life was about to be interrupted.

In those days, it was understood that for theology majors to get a call to ministry, they needed to have some experience canvassing door-to-door. I dreaded thinking about it. Kathy and I had married the year before, and we were barely making ends meet. Kathy had dropped out of college to work for an insurance company, and I had worked in construction that summer to pay for my tuition.

One Sunday afternoon, as we were enjoying a rare respite in our one-bedroom apartment, we got a call from my friend Bob Peck. He had canvassed the last two summers and was now student leader.

"Duane, the publishing directors are here recruiting students to canvass this summer," he said. "I'm going to be working near Lincoln. Would you be willing to canvass north of Lincoln?"

"No!" I said emphatically. I had other plans. Besides, Lincoln and the surrounding area had been overworked by other literature evangelists and was considered difficult.

"Come on, Duane, you know as a theology major you need to canvass," Bob insisted.

"No, I'm not going to do that," I said. "I can't. I have a good summer job in construction, and we need the income to pay my tuition for my senior year."

"Well, would you pray about it?" Bob said.

"No," I replied.

"Duane, you have to pray about it—you're going to be a pastor! You've got to."

"Okay," I finally agreed. "I guess we'll pray about it."

Kathy and Duane McKey as a young married couple.

I hung up the phone and told Kathy what Bob had said. We were both distraught. I was one year away from graduating, and if I did what Bob suggested, I wouldn't have the funds to graduate!

We decided to pray about it—after all, what else could we do? I said to Kathy, "The only way to know for sure if God wants me to canvass this summer and give up my good construction job is to draw straws."

Kathy was surprised, but I went to the kitchen cupboard, took out seven pieces of dry spaghetti, and said to Kathy, "Let's kneel down." Then I broke off one piece and held the seven pieces evenly for Kathy to pick.

"I'll pray and you draw the straw," I said. "If you draw the short piece of spaghetti, we will canvass. We'll give the Lord one chance out of seven. Six chances for us, and one for the Lord." I was convinced in my heart that there was no way the short one could be drawn!

So we prayed earnestly. I held the spaghetti tightly and Kathy pulled one out—it was the short one!

I was very upset. So I took all seven pieces and threw them in the trash. Then I went and got seven more. I broke one off and again we knelt down and prayed earnestly. I held out my hand to Kathy and she drew a second time—and it was the short one again!

Now we were convinced the Lord wanted me to canvass and sell Christian literature. Kathy said resignedly, "We're still young. If you don't sell enough to go back to college your senior year, we'll chalk it up to experience."

I agreed. I figured that if needed, I could stay out of school one year and work to get ahead.

So how did our summer turn out? Did God help us?

Did He ever! What an exciting time God had in store for us. And the construction company I had been working for went bankrupt that summer, so I would have been out of a job.

Bob and I had some wonderful experiences that summer. One time we were at a home doing canvassing with little success. The mother was distracted with her kids who kept running in and out, interrupting the presentation. I had everything laid out—the five books from the *Conflict of the Ages* series, plus an Arthur Maxwell *Bible Story* set.

Suddenly, the husband came home from work, and seeing us in his house shouted, "Who let them in here?" He was very upset and used some choice words. I immediately jumped up and shook his hand. He was a construction worker and I told him I had been one too. He sat down and I gave him the canvass. When I was finished, he wrote me a check for the whole lot! We were thrilled.

When I had a big sale like that, Kathy and I would celebrate by going to the nearby Dairy Queen for ice cream cones.

By the time the summer ended, the Lord had blessed in the most remarkable way. I had enough sales to pay not only all my tuition for my senior year, but most of Kathy's tuition as well, so she was able to return to school in the fall.

God taught me that being a real man—living on the edge for the adrenaline rush—can be had in a greater way by working for the Lord than by hanging on steel beams 20 feet off the ground! We learned that God is the God of the impossible. "He is able to do exceedingly abundantly above all that we ask or think." (Ephesians 3:20)

Many years have passed since this incredible experience. It was the first of many more throughout our years in ministry—because God is still in the business of miracles today! We've served in many places around the world—from the jungles of the African Congo to the concrete jungles of America—and what we've learned every time is that man's extremity is God's opportunity.

Every day we're bombarded by terrible news headlines—crimes, wars, human suffering and death—all fed to us on a daily basis. And often, weeks may pass without ever hearing any of God's news—the miracles taking place and the prayers being answered around the world. Many people sit in their pews every Sabbath thinking nothing is happening today in God's work.

But make no mistake about it, God is working like never before—and His miracles need to be shared! They should be our daily headlines. He calls us to "look at the nations, and watch, and be utterly amazed, for I am going to do something in your days that you would not believe, even if you were told." (Habakkuk 1:5)

That's why this book is about God's news—and His news is always good news! It's a short collection of some of the most amazing miracles taking place today through the worldwide ministry of Adventist World Radio.

I have seen God's providence through the years—some of which I also share here—but I've never before seen or heard the things I've been witnessing during the last few years as president of Adventist World Radio. This is no longer "business as usual," and it needs to be shared, because it will not only strengthen our faith, but it indicates that Jesus is coming soon.

So fasten your seatbelts as we review what God is doing. It's an amazing time to be alive, and I can't wait to see what God will do next!

Yours in the Blessed Hope,

Duane McKey
President

1
MIRACLE IN THE CONGO
The Experience That Changed My Ministry

FOR 20 YEARS, MISSIONARIES HAD BEEN WORKING in the Kasai region, an isolated area in the heart of the Congo, establishing a small mission station at Lulengele. Their years of toil and hardship had yielded a small Adventist church, a school, a medical dispensary and 300 converts.

Despite this small success, the missionaries were not content. The work was exploding in neighboring countries like Malawi, Zambia and Kenya—so why not in the Congo? Why not in this vast country right in the heart of Africa?

So the small band of missionaries began to pray, asking God to bless them exceedingly abundantly above all that they asked. They were doing all they could do, stretched to the max, so if something was going to change, God would have to intervene in some way.

Meanwhile, one day, the President of the Congo was driving with his entourage from the capital city of Kinshasa to the port city of Matadi. As they drove through the lowland hills, he began to notice something he hadn't noticed before, even though he'd made this trip hundreds of times.

A Congo stamp featuring President Mobutu Sese Seko.

There seemed to be churches everywhere, lots of them, and all had different names—the Church of the Prophet Simon, the Church of the Prophet Pierre, and the list went on. President Mobutu Sese Seko was not pleased. He asked,

"What is this? Who are these people, and where did all these churches come from?"

After some research, it was discovered that there were more than 1,000 different churches like this in the country. So a law was passed requiring all these churches to register with the Ministry of the Interior. For a church to be legally recognized in the Congo, the leader was required to have two qualifications:

1. He must have a college degree.

2. He must have at least $1,000 in the church's bank account.

If a church did not meet these requirements, then it would have to register under one of the 33 recognized churches in the Congo. The Adventist Church was already recognized in the Congo and was exempt from this process.

Soon, the office of the Ministry of the Interior was flooded with the "prophets" and leaders of these churches who were arriving to register their congregations. As it turned out, most of the 1,000 churches did not meet the necessary requirements.

As these leaders realized they must register and join a recognized church, they would approach the Minister of the Interior's secretary and ask him what they should do.

He would respond, "Back there on the table are the documents of the recognized churches. Read through them and decide which one you agree with. Then choose the one you like."

So the leaders would read and read and read, and then they would usually exclaim in frustration, "This is too confusing! Which church should we join?"

Now, let me pause here for a moment and tell you something about the Minister of the Interior's secretary. This young man was from the neighboring country of Rwanda, and the son of an Adventist pastor. Years before, he had left his beautiful mountain home and traveled for many days down the Congo

River to the steamy city of Kinshasa to pursue his studies there. After finishing his education, he got a job in the government and slowly drifted away from God, eventually leaving the Adventist Church. Years later, he became the Minister of the Interior's secretary in the Congo.

It's interesting how God arranges things, because He can see the end from the beginning, and just as He did with Joseph in Egypt, He places key people in our path that He knows will benefit His work.

This is exactly what happened in the Congo. When the leaders of the different churches would ask in confusion, "Which church should we join?" the young man would reply, "Well, depends. What do you believe?"

The reply was almost always the same: "We believe in everything that the Bible teaches!"

And the Minister of the Interior's secretary—this former Adventist pastor's son—would reply, "Well, in that case, if you are going to follow everything that is in the Bible, then you will have to become a Seventh-day Adventist!"

Just like that, almost overnight, entire congregations began coming to the Lulengele Mission asking to become Seventh-day Adventists. Our church went from only 300 members in 20 years to 100,000 new converts in six months! What our missionaries could not have accomplished on their own, God did for them!

This experience changed my life, because I was one of those missionaries. I spent my first years in the mission field of the Congo clearing these new converts for baptism. My task consisted of traveling through the Ituri Rainforest in the Kasai region, teaching and baptizing entire churches. It was an amazing experience. On one occasion, I walked through the forest for 17 days, drinking the local water and partaking of the local fare without falling ill—that was a miracle in itself!

When I say this experience changed my life, it's because it shaped my ministry. Every time I'm confronted with a new evangelistic challenge at Adventist World Radio—whether it's in Africa, India, Asia, Europe, or even in a Muslim country—I can't wait to see what God will do, because I know this is not our work, but His.

Sometimes we may be tempted to doubt our mission, our ability to finish the work or God's plan for our lives, but He *always* has a plan—and it's one far beyond what we can imagine or accomplish on our own.

Very soon, the earth will be lighted with the knowledge of truth (Revelation 18:1) and the preaching of the gospel will be finished. It may seem like an impossible task, and it is—but only if we think we're working alone. Because "He who began a good work in you (and me) will carry it on to completion until the day of Jesus Christ." (Philippians 1:6)

STOPPED AT THE BORDER!
The God of Lost Causes

"YOU NEED TO COME WITH US!" THE HEAVILY armed commander pointed to Pastor Borjan*, one of our Adventist World Radio leaders, and to a church elder who was with him. They had been sitting in a bus at a border crossing waiting to be cleared for entry into an undisclosed part of the world that is hostile to outsiders.

The commander had boarded the bus, and as he walked down the aisle, he had singled out Pastor Borjan and his companion. This was bad. The pastor had a small suitcase filled with 20 solar-powered radios, which were as many as they had dared carry with them. These radios were also audio players, known as Godpods. They held the entire Bible in audible form, plus a set of Bible studies in the local language. There were believers inside the country eagerly awaiting this precious cargo.

*Name changed for secrecy.

Looking at the luggage, the commander ordered that it be taken off the bus and placed on the ground for inspection. Then he noticed the small suitcase and asked, "Who does this belong to?"

Pastor Borjan's heart sank. Would their efforts be for naught? He began to pray.

"The suitcase is mine," he said as the commander ordered that all their luggage be picked up and that they follow him into the guardhouse.

One by one, their belongings were inspected, and when the commander opened the small suitcase, inside for all to see were rows of identical boxes containing the AWR radios.

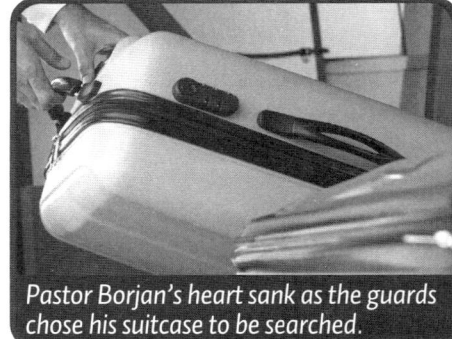

Pastor Borjan's heart sank as the guards chose his suitcase to be searched.

"You will have to pay a good tax on these since you will be selling them!" the commander said triumphantly.

"No, I won't be selling them," said Pastor Borjan. "I'm a Seventh-day Adventist pastor and work for Adventist World Radio. These radios are free as I share with others the good news of salvation. They contain messages of hope."

"Ha!" the commander scoffed. "Prove it to me!"

Pastor Borjan's fingers were shaking as he opened a box and took out a unit. He pushed a button, and the room filled with words from Scripture, followed by beautiful music and more Bible promises.

There was silence as everyone listened, and Pastor Borjan noticed tears rolling down the commander's face. Laying his gun against the wall, the commander said, "Pastor, I have no hope anymore. My country is in such a mess—what kind of a future can I give my children? You say these messages can bring me hope? What can I do to get one of these radios? I want to share it with my family and with my men."

By now, several more soldiers had joined them in the guardhouse, and when they realized what the tiny radios contained, some of them also began to cry, "Oh Pastor, please leave us two radios. We promise to listen. Our lives are not easy, and we need hope. People hate us, and we often have to do things we don't want to do. We need something good in our lives!"

Pastor Borjan couldn't believe it! These hardened men had been touched by the Holy Spirit. There was no other explanation. Taking out another small box, the pastor handed it to the commander and said, "These are precious radios. Please make good use of them. I pray they will bring you exactly what you need in your lives."

"Oh, thank you, thank you! Would you please pray for us?" The men quickly placed their guns next to the commander's and stood in a circle. Silent tears fell as Pastor Borjan and the elder prayed for these soldiers.

As they were leaving, the commander asked, "When will you be coming back? Here is my number. Call me. I want to make sure I'm on duty so I can talk to you again."

As Pastor Borjan and his companion boarded the bus, they couldn't help but marvel at what God had done. God's Spirit is at work everywhere. Sometimes we may feel we're working alone, but angels are the companions of all who go about God's business!

We are told that, "Angels that excel in strength are waiting to unite with human agencies. When His people shall be in greatest danger . . . God will work in their behalf. Man's extremity is God's opportunity." (*Selected Messages, Book 2*, p. 373)

What a wonderful promise! But this was not the end of the story. Pastor Borjan continued his journey inside the country and met with groups of believers who eagerly received the AWR radio Godpods. He also trained these believers to share the messages through their cell phones via WhatsApp.

SHARING HOPE THROUGH CELL PHONES

The Adventist Church in this undisclosed country organized church members into community service groups that went house to house helping people with their basic needs—from simple home repairs to yard work. They then prayed with them and asked if they would like to receive messages of hope from AWR through their cell phones. Amazingly, more than 37,000 people responded saying, "Yes! Please send me these messages of hope!"

Believers being trained for cell phone evangelism in this unnamed country.

THE DRUG CARTEL AND "THE OX"

Several months passed, and interest in the cell phone messages grew and spread like wildfire. We learned that in this unnamed country, there were 250 drug cartel members hiding in the mountains who wanted to meet Pastor Borjan. They had been receiving our AWR evangelistic sermons through WhatsApp on their cell phones and had many questions. These hardened drug lords now wanted to escape the prison of cartel life. They had found freedom in Jesus and wanted to be baptized into the Seventh-day Adventist Church!

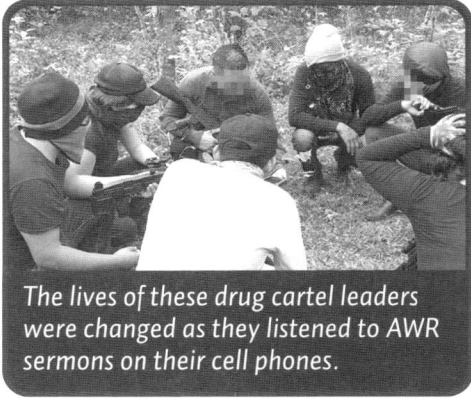

The lives of these drug cartel leaders were changed as they listened to AWR sermons on their cell phones.

Pastor Borjan decided to visit these men and made preparations to return. A few weeks before his trip to this restricted country, Pastor Borjan's phone rang. A very quiet voice on the other end said, "I only have two minutes. Is this the pastor who sends the audio messages of hope?"

"Yes," Pastor Borjan said.

"Well, listen carefully and don't say anything."

The man proceeded to tell Pastor Borjan that he was the commander in a well-organized anti-government force that had been creating chaos and terror for many years. "I've been listening to the audio messages and have many questions. Would you be willing to meet with me? I'll personally guarantee your safety."

Pastor Borjan was astonished. He swallowed hard before replying, "Certainly. I will be in your country soon and will meet with you."

It took no small miracle, but the day finally came when Pastor Borjan was able to travel to the undisclosed location to meet with this commander. Quickly offering a prayer for wisdom and protection, Pastor Borjan entered the room where this tall, powerful man stood. He immediately realized why they called him "The Ox"—he was an ox of a man!

His face was deeply lined by a life of hate and crime. Now at retirement age, he had been in this organization since he was 17 years old. After a few pointed questions to verify that he was indeed Pastor Borjan, the commander began to speak with a quiet voice of authority.

"I have never been a religious person and have lived an active life of crime. For most of my adult life, I have been unable to sleep much at night. All I do is replay in my mind the things I have done. I am not a good man."

For the next two hours, this powerful man confessed crime after crime. "Despite all this, when I began to receive the audio messages, I knew for the first time in my life that God is real, because as I listened to the messages, I had a strange sense of peace and of God's presence. I now sleep much better at night, but I would like you to pray for me. I simply can't believe that God can forgive me."

Pastor Borjan said, "Yes, you have done terrible things, but God's grace is greater than all our sins combined. He is able and willing to forgive you if you ask Him. He died for you even before you were born—before you committed your first crime."

They spoke into the wee hours of the morning as the general asked questions and received answers from God's Word.

A few weeks passed, and Pastor Borjan received another strange call. He didn't know the caller who said, "Do you remember the man you spoke with the last night you were here?"

Pastor Borjan was evasive, not knowing who was calling, but the man continued, "I'm talking about the man who said he didn't know if God could forgive him. Well, he now believes God has forgiven him and wants to be baptized!"

We were overjoyed at this news, and just a few weeks later, Pastor Borjan had the privilege of baptizing "The Ox" along with three other generals and 15 soldiers. They had exchanged their guns for a new life in Jesus. Before their baptism, they buried their guns, not wanting anyone else to use them again!

By now you may be thinking, *"What a beautiful ending!"* But wait . . . there's more!

"THE OX" – THE REST OF THE STORY

A little over a year had passed since Pastor Borjan's encounter with "The Ox." We hadn't heard from him since then, and all the AWR team could do was pray for him. Then one day, Pastor Borjan received a phone call from a soft-spoken woman whose voice he didn't recognize. She said, "Pastor, I'm the daughter of the man you know as 'The Ox'—the important man you baptized along with his friends. Do you remember him?"

Artist's representation.

Did he ever! Immediately, Pastor Borjan replied that he did, and this woman continued, "I'm calling to thank you for changing his life. You see, he was my father, and knowing Jesus made all the difference in his life. He found so much peace during this past year. Unfortunately, my dad just died of a heart attack, but before he passed away, he shared with me his AWR solar radio with all the presentations. He said he was praying for me, that I would find what he had found. I am now listening to the messages that changed his heart, and I called you because I want to say thank you for giving Jesus to my dad, because he passed this wonderful truth to me. He wanted me to experience what he had found."

It was a few moments before Pastor Borjan could speak again. There was a knot in his throat—not just for sadness at the death of this extraordinary man, but a quiet rejoicing that salvation had reached him just in the nick of time. This once-hardened criminal had not only found Jesus, but a desire had grown in his heart for the salvation of his own daughter, and that desire—that prayer of his heart—had been answered.

While this may seem like "The Ox's" final chapter—it's not really so, because for God's children, the best chapters are still ahead. Their works follow them, the ripple effects extending far and wide and for years to come . . . on into eternity.

THE MISSING TICKETS
The God of the Impossible

THROUGHOUT OUR YEARS IN MINISTRY, MY WIFE Kathy and I have experienced many miracles of God's providence. One such incident happened just at the start of our service in the mission field.

Our youngest was only six months old, and our eldest three, when we flew from New York to Geneva, Switzerland—our first transatlantic flight—and from there by land to Collonges-sous-Salève, France. The plan was to study French for six months before shipping out to the African jungle in the heart of the Congo.

When our studies were completed—and after some delays and postponements—we wrote to the General Conference letting them know we were ready, and asking them to send us the plane tickets for our trip to Africa.

To our surprise, the reply was not long in coming: "You already have the tickets. They were given to you with the rest of the paperwork."

This was serious. Back then, before the electronic age, a paper ticket was cash. If we lost those tickets, we would be losing our flight and thousands of dollars that could not be replaced. I asked Kathy, "Do you know where they might be?"

She said, "You know, some time ago I cleaned out everything. I think I may have thrown them away."

With a sinking feeling, we did another search of the apartment, but to no avail. The tickets were gone. Then we did the only thing we could do: we knelt down to pray, asking God for the impossible.

After the prayer, we decided to find out where all the city's trash was taken. But when we explained the reason, people were incredulous. "Are you serious?" they said. "Have you ever gone to the city dump? It's a mess—a junkyard with mountains and mountains of trash! It's impossible to retrieve anything once it's gone!"

We went anyway, and when we arrived at the site, we realized they were right. It seemed useless to even try to find anything in that huge field of foul-smelling discards. But we prayed again, asking God for the impossible.

When Duane and Kathy surveyed the mountain of trash, it seemed hopeless.

As we stood surveying the rotting mess, we noticed a pile of trash to the side, away from the rest. Then we recognized one of our children's toys, so we ran over, and that's when the impossible happened—we found the tickets! They were all there—all four of them!

We were so excited. Right then and there, amid the rubble, we thanked God for helping us find them. A few days later, we were on our way via Swiss Air to Kinshasa, then Lubumbashi, and then on to Lulengele Mission.

This incident at the start of our mission service was one of many that strengthened our faith, enabling us to face ever greater challenges.

A MODERN-DAY WITCH
"I Want Her Powerful Magic!"

COMMANDER LIAM* WAS IN CHARGE OF THE ARMED forces in a country under a dictatorship. He was a powerful, decorated commander who had complete control over all military operations of the government and carried out the wishes of the country's dictator.

The commander was many things, but "kind" was not a word that would come to mind if you met him. However, something interesting and unexpected happened. Someone began sending him messages of hope straight to his cell phone. These messages spoke of a God of love and forgiveness, a God who can change lives and knows the future, and especially a God who sent His Son to die for us and is coming again soon!

At first, Commander Liam was annoyed that someone had his private cell phone number and was sending these video presentations to him, but then he found out it was an acquaintance of his, and he decided to watch. Pretty soon he was hooked and fascinated by the series! You see, he was watching AWR's *Unlocking Bible Prophecies* with Cami Oetman, and each presentation was more compelling than the one before.

Commander Liam had many enemies, and was very aware of them, so to protect himself and his family, he hired a "witch" to cast spells on his enemies. She was known as a powerful witch, and he appreciated her help.

One day, as the commander was in his living room watching one of the video presentations, the witch strode in and said, "Stop! I need to talk to you!"

*Name changed for secrecy.

The commander put down his phone and waited. The witch said, "Who's sending you those videos, and who is that woman preaching? I can tell she has a magic more potent than mine!"

When the commander began sharing the content of the videos, the witch said, "I want some of that power, too! It brings me a strange sense of peace I haven't known before. Can you please tell the person sending you those videos to sign me up as well?"

As the commander watched Unlocking Bible Prophecies *on his mobile device, the witch commanded him to "Stop!"*

Today, Commander Liam and his witch are both listening to AWR's presentations and learning the full prophetic Adventist gospel message!

Truly, the messages from Adventist World Radio know no borders, no walls, no limits— and no dictatorships. God's Word is like a sharp sword that can penetrate to the soul in every corner of the world!

THE FORTUNE TELLER'S STORY
"Your Messages Are Interfering With My Channeling!"

CARMEN WAS A HIGHLY PRIZED FORTUNE teller—a medium who channeled spirits and was very good at predicting people's futures. Her appointment slots filled up daily as people sought her counsel on all matters of the heart, family and finances.

One day, someone began sending her cell phone messages through WhatsApp that talked about things she'd never heard before. They were AWR's *Unlocking Bible Prophecies* videos with Cami Oetman. She watched the presentations with interest, but her job kept her so busy that she didn't dwell long on them.

Then something odd began to happen. Carmen found that she had difficulty channeling the spirits. Then another scary symptom appeared—she couldn't predict people's futures anymore. This rattled her and she found herself having to fake her predictions and the supposed messages from the spirits. She couldn't understand it! This went on for a few days until it suddenly occurred to her that it had to be those messages she was receiving!

When Carmen started watching Unlocking Bible Prophecies, *she began having trouble channeling spirits and predicting the future.*

Artist's representation.

In a fit of anger, she threw down her cell phone and it skidded to a corner of the room. "I'm done with this!" she cried. "These messages are interfering with my channeling!"

The problem was that people texted her to request appointments, so she needed her cell phone. Reluctantly, she picked it up, and just then, a message popped up from the person who was sending her the presentations. It was a message of encouragement.

Carmen was so annoyed at this that she tried to swipe away the message, but it wouldn't budge, no matter how hard she tried. It stayed on her screen until she was finally forced to read it before she could delete it.

Every time she received text messages from her clients, she would pick up the phone, but if a sermon came on her screen, she couldn't get to her messages until she'd watched the whole presentation!

Carmen continued to schedule appointments and fake the channeling, but was terrified of getting caught. Finally, she decided to set aside some time, sit down, and listen to all the presentations together, from beginning to end. She needed to find out what power they held that was more powerful than that of the spirits.

As she listened to the presentations, her heart was stirred by new feelings she'd never felt before. She was drawn to Jesus by forces more powerful than those of the spirits she knew so well. By the time she finished watching all the presentations, she knew what she had to do. The words of Jesus uttered more than 2,000 years ago were fulfilled in Carmen when He said, "When I am lifted up from the earth, I will draw all people to myself." (John 12:32)

Carmen called her clients one by one and told them she would no longer be channeling for them. She could no longer practice divination or palm reading, no longer read tea leaves or use Tarot cards. She had not yet received full Bible instruction on these subjects, but she understood there were two very different spirits at work: the Spirit of God and the spirit of darkness, and they were incompatible.

Carmen contacted the cell phone evangelist who had been sending her the messages, and he invited her to an in-depth Bible study. She accepted Jesus as her Savior and gave her life to Him. Soon after, Carmen was baptized into the Seventh-day Adventist Church. "I feel a joy in my heart I have never felt before," she said. "Jesus is now my Friend, and His Spirit is the only one I channel now."

MY MOTHER'S PRAYER
The AK-47 Was Pointing Directly at Me!

THE YEAR WAS 1976 AND WE WERE MISSIONARIES IN the Congo, stationed in the Kasai Province. There were warring factions in the Congo and unrest in neighboring countries. I was returning from a trip to Nairobi, Kenya, anxious to get home to my wife and children, but car problems delayed me and I stopped for the night at a village near the border.

I had slept in my car for about an hour when a noise outside awoke me. Surrounding the car were 20 soldiers, all pointing their AK-47s directly at me. This was bad. People tended to disappear in such encounters. The leader demanded that I get out, and I tried to explain that I was an American missionary and reached over to show him my passport, but he shouted for me to stop, and I heard all 20 machine guns being cocked. In that moment, I thought my life would end. They took me to their headquarters, and then—inexplicably—let me go!

A few years later, back in America, I shared my story at a church in Oregon and sent a copy of the recording to my parents, who were dairy farmers in Oklahoma. My mother wanted to know the exact date and time of that incident. When I told her, she knew why they'd let me go. One night, she'd awakened from a deep sleep terribly distressed for my safety. She'd knelt and fervently prayed for me for almost an hour, until peace returned to her heart. When looking at the dates, we realized she had prayed just hours before my fateful encounter.

7
THE WITCH COW THIEF
"Why Can't I Kill Them When I've Killed So Many?"

ALFRED WAS A FEARED COW THIEF IN A dangerous part of Madagascar called the Red Zone. Known as a Dahalo, a cow thief must also be a witch, and Alfred was a powerful one. Witchcraft is supposed to protect cow thieves from anything metal, including guns and knives, and allows them to kill their enemies.

Alfred had a neighbor named Michel, a Seventh-day Adventist and a faithful Adventist World Radio listener. Alfred hated Michel's religion, and one day about three years ago, he decided to kill Michel and his family with witchcraft incantations. He had killed many people like this before and saw no problem in doing it again. But to his great surprise, when he attempted to kill Michel, nothing happened!

Every day, he watched Michel and his family go about their business as usual. None of them died—they didn't even get sick! This greatly disturbed him. He thought, "Why can't I kill them when I've killed so many?"

His frustration grew, and he decided he needed to know more about Michel's religion. He began to listen carefully whenever Michel talked about the Bible.

Michel was well-aware that Alfred had tried to kill him and his family, but that didn't change his attitude toward him. He continued loving and respecting him. This attitude touched Alfred's heart, so he began coming over to Michel's house every day to listen to AWR with Michel and his family! Then, before he realized what was happening, Alfred was attending a Bible study class.

Despite his interest, he did his best to avoid meeting the Adventist pastor, but he did decide to begin keeping the Sabbath. When AWR shared several Godpods in his village, Alfred managed to get one and listened to it constantly. There was one question that kept nagging at him, and he was searching for the answer: "Why is my power so weak against Michel's God?"

Slowly, the truth began to dawn on him: He had been wrong his whole life, both in his beliefs, and in his actions. When he finally understood this, he felt so ashamed!

Then the South West Malagasy Adventist Conference organized an AWR Godpod listening group—and not only was Alfred among them, but he was the first one to arrive on opening night! As God's Spirit worked on his heart, Alfred put away all practices of witchcraft, and when the time came to respond to the call to give his heart and his life to Jesus, he responded without hesitation.

Alfred was baptized shortly thereafter, and is now the oldest and most faithful member of the Seventh-day Adventist church in Ankilivalokely, Madagascar. His family followed him, and all are now Seventh-day Adventists!

Upon seeing this, his friends wanted to know, "Who is this God who convinced this great man to become a faithful Adventist Christian?"

Alfred's testimony has led many of his friends and family to accept Jesus. The gospel continues to spread in the Red Zone, and the small group of Adventists in Alfred's village is working to build a church.

THE CAN OPENER THAT DIDN'T WORK
When God Stopped a Can Opener

IT WAS 1984 AND WE WERE BACK IN THE CONGO after two years in America. I needed to make a trip to South Africa to buy supplies and purchase a new truck for the mission station, so we decided to make it a family trip, and my wife, Kathy, and our two children came with me. It was Friday afternoon when we arrived at Victoria Falls and decided to camp there for the Sabbath.

We had a wonderful Sabbath together, and in the afternoon, as it was getting hot, we parked the van in the shade, opened the windows, and took a nap until the heat of the day abated. I awoke from my nap to see someone sticking their arm in the front window and snatching our video camera. I jumped out, yelling at him as he ran away, and he dropped the camera and ran into the bush.

We praised God for protecting our things and enjoyed the rest of the Sabbath without incident.

The next morning, we decided to splurge for breakfast by opening a can of Veja-Links® we had brought from America. But when I tried to open the can, the can opener wouldn't work, no matter how hard I tried. Finally, I told Kathy to get my small army can opener from the briefcase in the back of the van. She went to look for it, but there was no briefcase.

That's when we realized the thief from the day before had also stolen our briefcase! This was serious, because inside was the cashier's check for $50,000 to purchase the new truck, plus my passport and countless letters that had been given to me to mail from South Africa.

Though it seemed fruitless, we searched the area, but nothing turned up. We prayed earnestly, asking God to protect the mission funds. Then I remembered hearing that sometimes when people steal something like a briefcase, they dump the incriminating contents as soon as possible. So we kept searching. I walked along the Zambezi River above the falls, and there, under a tree, I saw some papers. I ran over, and the contents of my briefcase were scattered on the ground! All the envelopes had been opened and searched. All of them, that is, except the envelope with the cashier's check. It was still intact with the check inside. I also found my passport under some papers.

But for the can opener, we wouldn't have realized the briefcase was missing until it was too late. God has a way of taking care of His things and of His people! It's a lesson I've never forgotten.

Many years and many more miracles later, God brought us to Adventist World Radio and some of our most exciting challenges yet.

THE AWR CHICKENS
Can Chickens Be Converted?

SOMETIMES WE HEAR STORIES THAT JUST MAKE US smile and praise God. And this is one of them.

A chicken farmer on the island of Mindoro, Philippines, was having trouble with his chickens. They just weren't laying eggs. Someone suggested he contact a chicken psychologist and ask him to evaluate his hens. So, he did, and after examining the birds, the expert concluded the chickens were stressed. He advised the farmer to buy some radios and place them around the chicken cages, assuring him that music would help the hens lay more eggs.

So the farmer did just that. He tuned the radios to his favorite music station and waited to see what would happen. It was a disaster. The rock music stressed the chickens even more, and they stopped laying eggs altogether.

When he went back to the psychologist, the man suggested the farmer find a different station with better music. So the farmer began searching for a different station. As he turned the dial, he came upon our AWR station and liked

As the farmer played the AWR station on his radio, the chickens resumed laying eggs.

Duane McKey, AWR President

what he heard, so he decided to try it. In no time, the hens started laying eggs again.

He was very happy with this result, but then our radio station began airing the *Unlocking Bible Prophecies* series with Cami Oetman, so there was less music, but the chickens doubled their production! They seemed to enjoy Cami's soothing voice. And when the series ended, the station began airing AWR's *Earth's Final Countdown* series. I know my voice is not as smooth as Cami's, but they continued with their egg production uninterrupted!

That in itself was a miracle, but the real miracle came afterward. You see, not only were the chickens listening, but the farmer was listening as well. God was working on his heart, and he was convicted of the truth. He called our radio station and requested baptism.

FOUR GALLONS OF GLUE
"My God Shall Supply All Your Needs…"

FOR OUR MOVE TO THE CONGO, WE WERE TOLD TO pack our things in 50-gallon drums and then weld them shut. This was to prevent our goods from being stolen and to keep them dry while being transported across the ocean by ship.

We were also instructed to buy plastic bag liners to line the drums. I looked everywhere near our home in Nebraska, but it seemed no one carried such large bags. Someone suggested that I check with local mortuaries, but that didn't appeal to us.

Then we got a lead that a furniture factory had drums we could get almost for free. So I had the drums transported to the house, but we still had no large bags. Then one day Kathy said, "Why don't we look inside the drums?"

We opened them, and to our surprise, inside each drum was a large plastic bag. This was just what we needed, except that at the bottom of each bag was a thick layer of white liquid. We were dismayed, thinking the bags were contaminated, but upon investigation, we learned the white liquid was wood glue. Kathy suggested we collect the glue in plastic gallon milk jugs. By the time we were finished, we had four gallons of wood glue.

Months later, after first attending a language school in France, we finally arrived at the Lulengele Mission in Central Zaire (now the Congo). Thankfully, our drums were there waiting for us, as we were thousands of miles from anywhere—four hours by plane from our mission office to the nearest major city of Lubumbashi! Our little mission plane dropped us off and we stayed there until it took us out. It's also where we witnessed the miracle I share in the opening story of this book, where 100,000 were converted by a miracle of God's intervention.

One of the first things we learned when we arrived was that two mission homes were being constructed—one of them for us—and the carpenters needed wood glue to be able to put the doors and cabinets together. There was no glue to be found in the middle of the jungle. What could they do?

We have learned that God will supply your needs before you even know what to ask for!

Guess what? God had anticipated our need. Before we'd asked, before we even knew to ask, He had answered. We had all the glue that was needed! That's when I learned that God is able to do exceedingly abundantly above all that we ask or think. And that even before we call, He will answer, and while we are yet speaking, He will hear. (Isaiah 65:24)

MOHAMMED AND THE IMAM
"Your Young Men Shall See Visions..."

FOR MANY YEARS, ADVENTIST WORLD RADIO HAD been trying to make inroads into a Muslim geographic cluster called the "Stan" countries: Afghanistan, Kazakhstan, Kyrgyzstan, Pakistan, Tajikistan, Turkmenistan and Uzbekistan.

There was no Adventist presence in one of those countries (which must remain unnamed), and we thought we were having no success with our shortwave broadcasts despite our efforts. That is, until recently, when we received the following story.

THE UNUSUAL DREAM

One night, Mohammed had a vivid dream. He dreamed that he heard a voice telling him to come out of the darkness and into the light.

In the Middle East, people from Islamic backgrounds believe in dreams and visions much more than those in the Western world. This dream troubled Mohammed. He asked his wife about it, but she didn't know what it could mean. The only other person he could think to ask was his father. So Mohammed shared the dream with him.

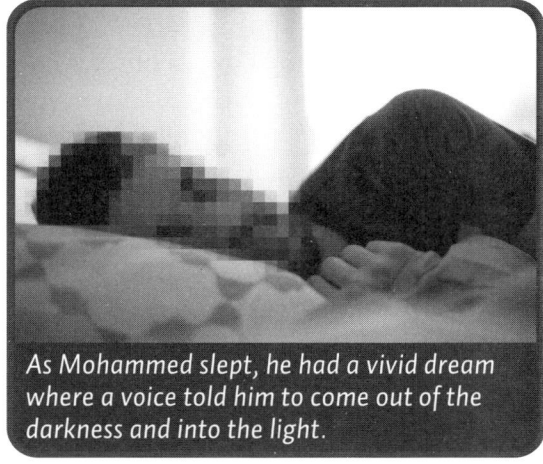

As Mohammed slept, he had a vivid dream where a voice told him to come out of the darkness and into the light.

Unbeknownst to Mohammed, almost two years before, his parents had been listening to the radio one day when they lost the radio signal. As they turned the dial searching for their program, they came across one of our broadcasts intended for the country of Iran. The languages are similar, so Mohammed's parents understood the message.

They enjoyed it so much that they began listening regularly. Eventually, they contacted the radio station and began receiving Bible studies. As a result, the year before, Mohammed's parents had been baptized—the first two people we're aware of who became Seventh-day Adventists in that country!

Mohammed's parents were regularly meeting with a group of people to study the Bible.

Meanwhile, Mohammed had no idea about this. The penalty for becoming a Christian is so severe in that part of the world, that everything is done in secrecy. So when Mohammed approached his father and shared his dream—asking for the meaning—his father surprised him by saying, "I know exactly what your dream means. The voice you heard is the voice of Jesus. He wants you to accept Him. You must become a Seventh-day Adventist."

Wow! Mohammed was shocked. But then a memory came to him from 15 years before. He'd known a nurse who was a Seventh-day Adventist. He remembered how different she was, and how she exuded joy and peace. It had affected him in a strange way back then, and he'd always wanted to know more about what she believed. Now was his chance!

Mohammed's father gave him a Bible, and together they studied with an Adventist pastor from a neighboring country. As a result, a few months later, two AWR team members traveled to an undisclosed location to witness the baptism of both Mohammed and his wife!

We were amazed by what God had done. But He was not finished—because that's not the end of the story!

THE MUSLIM IMAM

Mohammed learned that his parents were regularly meeting with a group of people, and they were studying the Bible together. Since their baptism, the group had been steadily growing until there were 80 people meeting and studying together. How were they finding people interested in studying the Bible? With extreme caution! The group lives in the middle of Taliban territory, and the danger is so high that even Mohammed didn't know about his parents' conversion until he confided his dream to them.

After his baptism, Mohammed knew that the danger for him was even higher than for other people. You see, Mohammed's wife's father is an imam—a Muslim religious leader. These men are not only highly respected, but also feared. What would the imam do if he found out his daughter had become a Christian? Mohammed and his wife lived in fear of this and were always very careful.

Then the unexpected happened.

One day, Mohammed's wife was visiting her family when they began talking about Abraham. Muslims are descendants of Abraham through Ishmael—the son of Abraham and Sarah's maid—so they claim Abraham as their father just as much as Jews do. However, most of what has been written about Abraham comes from Jewish writings and the Bible, so their knowledge from Islamic writings is limited.

As the family discussed the life of Abraham—mostly from hearsay—Mohammed's wife found herself filling in tidbits here and there from her Bible readings.

This happened several times on several occasions, until one day her father, the imam, pulled her aside and said, "There is only one way you can know these stories from the Bible. You're studying to be a Christian, aren't you?"

Mohammed's wife was alarmed, and for a moment considered denying it, but then she felt that God was asking her to be courageous. She said, "Yes, Father, I am."

The imam then asked, "Do you have a Bible?" And she replied that she did.

That's when her father said something that amazed her: "Bring it with you the next time you come so that we can study together."

Isn't that amazing? That's God's Spirit working in ways we don't understand behind these seemingly impenetrable walls! God's Word through the airwaves truly knows no walls, no borders and no limits!

Both Mohammed and his wife lost their lucrative jobs in healthcare when it was noted that he no longer prayed toward Mecca five times a day. They are looked at with suspicion, but they are not discouraged. We hope to begin a health clinic in their area that can be a beacon of light.

Mohammed and his wife believe—as do we—that there are thousands of people in this cluster of "Stan" countries who are ready to accept Jesus but are just too afraid to come forward. We recently began broadcasting into their country in their own dialect. Our *Revelation of Hope* sermons have already been translated, and we can't wait to see what God will do next!

"ALEXA" SHARES THE TRUTH
Can a Virtual Assistant Lead Someone to the Truth?

RECENTLY, MICHAEL, THE RADIO MANAGER IN OUR North England radio station, received a surprising message on live chat that he said "carried the characteristic British soft-spoken mannerism":

> *I agree with what your church presents and would like to join if I may? I would like details on how to join your church, please? —Rob*

When Michael contacted Rob, it just so happened that it was Rob's birthday. He was turning 73 that day and was moved that our response had arrived on his special day. He believed it was no accident—that it was God giving him a birthday gift!

Michael soon learned that Rob, now retired, was once a high-ranking official in the British army. Due to an unfortunate injury, he was now also blind. Michael asked him, "How did you, being blind, find our radio station?"

Rob then told the following story:

One day he asked Alexa, his virtual assistant, to find a radio station for him. Alexa immediately tuned to a station that was broadcasting a sermon. After listening for a while, Rob asked Alexa what station was playing. She replied it was Adventist Hope Radio—our AWR radio station in northern England!

Rob enjoyed it so much that he continued listening and made it his go-to station. For two years, he listened to a variety of sermons and presentations, until one day he felt he couldn't wait any longer—he had to belong to the group of people who put out these programs! That's when he sat down and composed the message Michael received.

Soon after, Michael had the opportunity to visit Rob—who lives in Skegness, a seaside town in England. It's about three hours away from our station in Birmingham, close to the Scottish border.

"I came away blessed from the visit," said Michael. "Here is a man who has seen and experienced much in his life. I sensed no regret, but instead, an overwhelming sense of one who has experienced God's touch of grace and forgiveness—one extremely appreciative of God's very presence in his life."

Rob has recently started a small Bible study group in his home and soon plans to be baptized in the local Seventh-day Adventist Church.

What an amazing story! God sees the hearts of sincere souls wherever they may be—even in a remote corner of England. And if Jesus said the stones could speak the truth, He can certainly use Alexa—and Adventist World Radio—to accomplish His bidding!

AN UNEXPECTED RESPONSE

After the Alexa experience, the staff at our AWR radio station in northern England began to think: If God can do that without us doing anything, how much more could He do if we decided to do more?

Inspired by this small success (which really wasn't small at all!), they began to think about what more they could do. They decided to reach out to the listening audience and offer Bible studies to all who were interested. They expected a very limited response, if any at all.

Imagine their shock and surprise when 2,500 people responded requesting Bible studies! This was so unexpected that their small staff was left with the logistics of tending to all the requests.

This is the kind of problem we love to have! Isn't God amazing? It reminds me of a quote written many years ago by Ellen White that I believe is very close to being fulfilled: "I saw the latter rain was coming as suddenly as the midnight cry, and with ten times the power." (*Manuscript 4*, 1852)

IN A HURRY TO DIE!
The Radio That Wouldn't Work

NATHAN HAD DECIDED HE WAS GOING TO COMMIT suicide. His girlfriend, whom he loved more than life itself, had left him for another man the week before, and, devastated, he'd sought refuge in drugs and alcohol to dull the pain. But peace eluded him, and he hadn't eaten or slept in days, unable to focus on his work.

He'd finally reached the conclusion that he didn't want to live anymore. Getting into his car, he sped at 120 mph up a mountainside, intent on careening over the side and into a precipice. That would be the best way, he decided. As he drove at breakneck speed, his car radio was blaring heavy metal music, its din matching the turmoil in his mind.

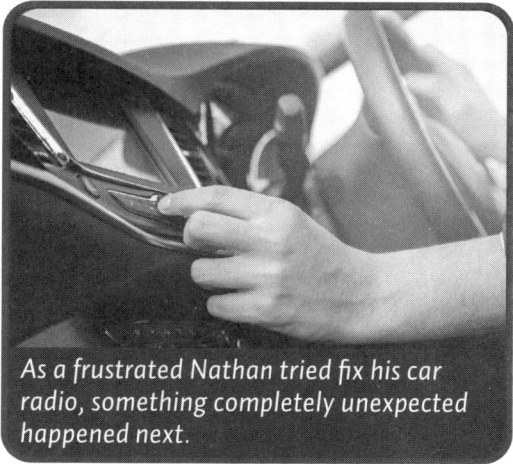

As a frustrated Nathan tried fix his car radio, something completely unexpected happened next.

Suddenly, the radio went dead, and silence filled the car. This made

Nathan furious, and he banged on the dashboard to get it to come back on. At first, nothing happened, and his frustration mounted. In exasperation, he gave the radio a final bang, and that's when he heard it come back on. But it was not the station he had been listening to. It was Adventist Radio London, and a man was speaking about peace and hope in Christ.

Nathan was so shocked that he stopped the car and stared at the radio. He sat there listening to the entire message—a sermon on hope that seemed to be meant just for him.

At the end of the message, a phone number was given, and Nathan called it.

"How can I help you?" a kindly voice answered.

"I need hope, I need love and I need Christ," Nathan managed to say.

He was immediately put in contact with one of the local Adventist pastors, John Melki, and Nathan's spiritual journey began. As he studied with Pastor Melki, he felt a deep sense of gratitude at what God had done for him. His suicidal thoughts vanished, and at the end of the studies, he was baptized into the Chelmsford Adventist Church. Now he works on a project with the homeless in the city, leading them to Christ and to a better life.

14

MIRACLE IN MALIBU
A Providential Encounter

LET ME SHARE A STORY FROM ONE OF OUR volunteer AWR Ambassadors. They have one of the best jobs in the world: to share with others the miracles God is working through AWR. That's it—just share the stories! You may have met one of them at your local church, because we feel that if God is working through AWR, we have to share the miracles!

Often, we may think that miracles only happen in the mission field—in the remote corners of the world—so let me share one Ambassador's story right here in America:

It was a beautiful morning in Malibu, California, when Judith went with some members from the Malibu Adventist Church to canvass the neighborhood and pass out AWR DVDs with some of our miracle stories.

They were in the Malibu shopping center when Judith and her friends noticed two ladies sitting on a bench. One of the church members approached one of them and said, "Good morning. I just felt impressed to come up and say that God loves you so much and He's coming soon! Oh, and by the way, not sure if you know this, but the true day of worship is Saturday, according to the Bible."

How is that for an opener? But you know, God takes anything we do with a sincere heart, and His Spirit works on the heart of the receiver. What happened next surprised everyone.

The lady's eyes grew wide, and she brought her hand up to her chest as she exclaimed, "Are you Seventh-day Adventists?"

"Yes," Judith and her friends replied. Then the lady told them the following story:

"I'm from San Diego, and I drove all the way up here for the weekend to get away and have some peace. Oh, I just wanted a little peace. I've been searching for peace—I want to find it so badly!"

Judith and her friends were astounded. Then the lady asked, "Where is your church?" And after the ladies gave her the address, she said, "I've been a backslider for more than 20 years and God found me here in Malibu. I want to come back to God and join the Malibu Adventist Church!"

Wow! When I heard this story, I knew I had to share it, because it proves once again that when we venture out and do something for Jesus, God's Spirit is there! It doesn't matter whether it's in the far corners of the world, or right here in America! But nothing will happen if we do nothing. We have to give God a chance, and when we do, He will exceed our expectations!

ANIL AND HIS ATHEIST FRIEND
"And Before They Call, I Will Answer..."

SOME TIME AGO I SPOKE WITH PASTOR ANIL Kanda, who grew up in a Sikh family living right here in America. Through a set of providential circumstances, someone shared with him the gospel and our distinct prophetic Adventist message. He embraced it wholeheartedly and felt the calling to be a pastor.

Early one morning, during his personal devotional time, he read a Bible passage that he liked, and as was his custom, he immediately sent it to several people on his WhatsApp list with whom he shares inspirational messages. But that particular morning, he made a mistake. He hit the "send" button before realizing he'd included an atheist friend who always chided him for his beliefs. This friend had once been a Christian, but had long-since stopped believing.

Too late, Anil noticed the mistake. The message had already gone out and could not be retrieved. He waited, looking at his phone and wondering what his friend would say, probably upset at being disturbed so early in the morning with what he normally called "nonsense."

To his surprise, seconds later the reply came back: "Thank you, brother."

This was so amazing, coming from his friend, that he had to call him and ask what he meant. That's when his friend told him the following story:

> "I had just woken up from a dreadful dream, where all I could feel was a dark sense of nothingness, aloneness and despair. The lingering impression from the dream was so terrible, that I cried out, 'If there is a God, please help me and show yourself!'
>
> In that instant, my phone pinged, and the message I saw read, 'And before they call, I will answer, and while they are yet speaking, I will hear.'" (Isaiah 65:24)

It was the message Anil had just sent! With joy in his heart, Anil heard his friend say, "Now I know there is a God!"

16
THE UNEXPECTED EVANGELIST
When God Works Outside Our Box

ANOTHER INCREDIBLE PHONE CALL WE RECENTLY received was from Pastor Luis Duran from Mexico. He helps with our cell phone evangelism in much of Latin America and told us the most amazing story!

He recently conducted a cell phone evangelism training in one of the Adventist churches in Mexico. Several people signed up to be cell phone evangelists and receive the weekly presentations for distribution. Every week, Luis sent out the sermons to the group he had trained, and they, in turn, shared them with others.

One day, Luis received a text message from one of the cell phone evangelists asking a question that didn't make sense to Luis. It was something that every Adventist would know. But he texted the answer anyway and sat back, thinking about the odd exchange.

Then, on an impulse, Luis texted again, "Out of curiosity, which church is your home church?"

The cell phone evangelist replied, and when Luis read the message, he was completely floored! It said:

> "I attend an evangelical church. I am not an Adventist, but I was just visiting the Adventist church the day you had the cell phone evangelism training, so I

stayed for the whole day. I took notes and then went back to my church and started sending out the sermons you provided. I've already trained several people to share them with family and friends as well. We get together as a group each week and spend time discussing that week's presentation and studying together.

We've loved the emphasis on prophecy, since we didn't know anything about that before. We had to accept that our views on the state of the dead have been incorrect. The only thing that has caused some disagreement and discussion has been on the topic of the Sabbath. Oh, and by the way, I've also been sending the presentations to the leaders of the evangelical pastors' alliance here in the city. I would love for us all to get together with you sometime soon."

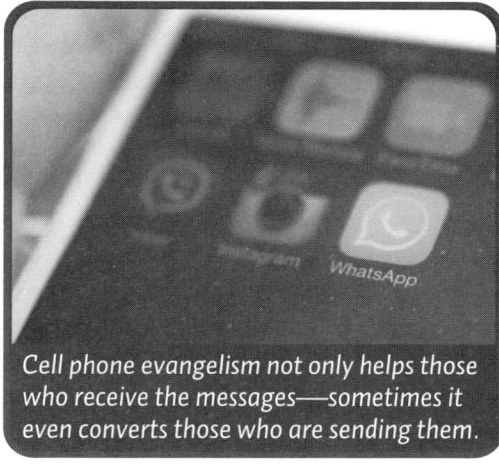

Cell phone evangelism not only helps those who receive the messages—sometimes it even converts those who are sending them.

Isn't that amazing? This is not our work. God can take what you and I do and just run with it! He is working in the hearts of people like never before, rewarding our efforts above all we can ask or think!

THE UNUSUAL VISITOR
No Chance Encounter

ONE OF OUR AWR COORDINATORS FOR INDIA HAD just concluded an evangelism training session for the day when he saw a man approaching. The man looked extremely poor, even by Indian standards, and our coordinator, Tim, got the impression that this man was coming to ask for money.

However, the man surprised him by requesting prayer for his eight-year-old daughter. She had a hole in her heart, and the father was taking her to a hospital in the city. The man's wife stood just behind him holding a baby, and what struck Tim was that she wore none of the jewelry that is common among Indian women.

After prayer, the man seemed to blend into the crowd, so Tim called out to him through his interpreter, asking if there was anything else he needed. The man said no, except that if Tim were ever in his village for a seminar—several hundred miles away—he would have 10 pastors come and listen to his presentations.

Believing him to be an Adventist pastor, Tim explained he would need an invitation from the local conference to visit that district. That's when the interpreter said, "I don't think he's Adventist."

Sure enough, Tim learned the man was a Pentecostal pastor. But what was such a pastor doing in an AWR training session? Tim's interest was piqued, and he looked more closely at the little family. He noticed their heavy looks of care and weariness, especially from the man's wife, and felt impressed he should invite them to eat.

But when he did, the man declined the invitation, and when Tim insisted, the man declined again, even as he and his wife were leaving.

In that moment, Tim thought of Abraham's invitation to the three angels before the destruction of Sodom and Gomorrah. In the book *Patriarchs and Prophets,* we read that the three angels initially declined Abraham's invitation to stop and eat. The patriarch had to insist before they accepted. Tim later told me, "I cannot describe the surreal sense that came over me as I, too, insisted this man come and join me for a meal. And he finally agreed, saying 'I will come and eat with you.'"

Let me share in Tim's own words what happened next:

> *"When I had first arrived in India, the conference had lodged me in a beach-front resort hotel that was absolutely beautiful with landscaped grounds and a white sandy beach. I decided to treat this family at the restaurant of that hotel. We traveled there in the local church vehicle, and when we arrived and went inside, there was no doubt this family looked out of place. In fact, as we later learned, in all their life of poverty, they could never have hoped to even enter such an establishment.*
>
> *Since it wasn't quite time to eat yet, I led the family to the back and showed them the beauty of the grounds. I will never forget their faces. The look of care and toil seemed to vanish, and the most beautiful, joyous smiles appeared as they realized that as our guests, all this was for them to enjoy. Grabbing their children, they rushed off to enjoy the magnificence of the place.*
>
> *Returning later, Pastor Nayak (for that was his name) sat down with me and I shared with him (through my pastor interpreter) the Three Angels' Messages and the Sabbath. As I concluded, the man broke down crying saying, 'God has led me here.'*
>
> *After a delicious meal, we sent them on their way. We later learned that upon arriving at the hospital, the doctors performed tests on the little girl, only to discover that the hole in her heart was gone. She had been healed!"*

What a wonderful testimony! But the story doesn't end there! Because we had Pastor Nayak's contact information, and soon we invited him to another AWR training event in another state. He came and learned more fully the Bible truths for our time, including the Sabbath truth.

Pastor Nayak's background was Hindu, and before accepting Christ, he had worshiped other "gods" in demon-inspired ceremonies. His family had been well-off, but when he accepted Jesus as his Savior to become a Pentecostal minister, he had been shunned by his family and had left his prior life and any wealth that could have come with their association, accepting the life of poverty to walk with Jesus.

Now, as the conviction of truth was presented to him, he responded by saying, "I have given up everything for Jesus. How can I not follow Him in this, the Sabbath truth, as well?"

Pastor Nayak returned from the AWR meeting equipped with a projector and the *Revelation of Hope* sermons to teach his people the truths he had learned. Arrangements were soon made for an AWR evangelist to visit him and his three congregations and help him teach his people. Then, we received word that Pastor Nayak and his wife wanted to be baptized as Seventh-day Adventists. We were overjoyed!

I invited Pastor Nayak and his family to come to Chennai when the AWR team was visiting India, and had the joy of personally witnessing their baptism. The words of John 10:16 kept resonating in my mind, *"And I have other sheep which are not of this fold: them also I must bring, and they shall hear my voice."*

Pastor Nayak and his wife (in white) on the day of their baptism share their joy with Duane McKey and Cami Oetman.

18
THE ENCOUNTER AT TAITA FALCON LODGE
A God-Ordained Appointment

THERE IS A CHRISTIAN SONG THAT IS SUNG IN South Africa that repeats over and over the words, *"Why, Why, Why . . ."* That is what I was saying to my wife, Kathy, as we bounced over the rough road on our way to the hotel outside of Livingstone, Zambia. Why had we chosen lodging we knew nothing about, and now were being jostled about over an incredibly rough road for almost an hour?

It would be 36 hours later when we would discover the answer and know why God had orchestrated it all.

The week had started on a high note. We had been in the capital city of Lusaka, Zambia, for an AWR evangelism planning meeting with the Zambian Union leadership and the Lusaka pastors. By the time the meetings had ended, we were excited. The pastors had just pledged to have an unprecedented 1,000 evangelistic meetings right there in the city—all at the same time!

We had returned to our hotel and proceeded to make a reservation for our next stop, this time in Livingstone, to plan additional evangelistic meetings. We had tried every hotel available but found them fully booked.

Finally, after much searching, we had found a lodge with some vacancies. The website said they were located "a short distance" outside Livingstone, and we were so relieved to find a room that we immediately made a reservation.

After arriving at the airport, we started the drive to the lodge, and the road was fine until we turned off the pavement onto an extremely rough side road. We bounced and bounced, and after almost an hour of this, I wondered if we'd ever arrive as the car advanced into the bush with no civilization in sight. To make matters worse, it was dark, which made it seem like an even longer journey.

After what felt like forever, we saw the lights from the Taita Falcon Lodge. To our relief, as we arrived, we were met by a very kind hotel manager and a few of the staff. The manager, Antoinette, made us feel right at home in this out-of-the-way place.

The next morning, we discovered why God had led us there. We woke up to a beautiful view outside our window, with the fast-flowing Zambezi River just below Victoria Falls. When we went down to breakfast, we were surprised to see Antoinette sitting at the bar reading from a Bible—and smoking!

"I just love studying Bible prophecy," she said.

This was startling and unexpected, and as you can imagine, a conversation-starter. We were even more surprised when she explained that her uncle was a Seventh-day Adventist, and every Sabbath sent an email with spiritual content to family and friends.

Antoinette said she always read her uncle's messages, and soon began to ask him questions. He referred her to a man in Namibia called Neville Neveling, who had just begun a series of virtual evangelistic meetings via WhatsApp.

Antoinette signed up to receive his messages and soon began studying things she had never heard before. The more she studied, the more she realized that what she had been taught was wrong and not what the Bible says.

One day, after one of the lessons, she said to her husband, "Did you know we were taught wrong? Saturday is the Sabbath and not Sunday. We've been going to church on the wrong day."

To her surprise, his response was, "I know. I learned that years ago."

After breakfast, Antoinette and her husband gave us a ride back to town on that bumpy road again, but this time it didn't seem quite as daunting in the daylight, and we enjoyed a lovely conversation with them.

We had a busy day in Livingstone with pastors and leaders as we made evangelism plans for the following year, and thankfully, accomplished everything on our list that day. Then we headed back for the third time over the rough road!

The next morning, just before checking out, Kathy went to thank Antoinette for her hospitality. Just then, the local pastor arrived to take us across the border to the town of Victoria Falls in Zimbabwe. We introduced him to Antoinette, who insisted we return for another visit in the future. The pastor agreed, and suggested we could hold meetings in the nearby village. Antoinette was delighted with the idea. We finally parted ways with promises to return and meet again.

As we drove to Victoria Falls, I couldn't stop thinking about the man Antoinette said was sending out Bible messages. Neville's name sounded familiar, but I didn't know why. I wanted more information on the cell phone evangelism he was doing. Antoinette had given me his phone number, so I called him, and like Paul Harvey used to say, here is the rest of the story . . .

HOW IT ALL BEGAN

Neville had been working at fine-tuning his cell phone ministry for four years. He had a background in radio and TV broadcasting, as well as in computer technology, and was able to set up a virtual church for Afrikaans-speaking people of Dutch descent.

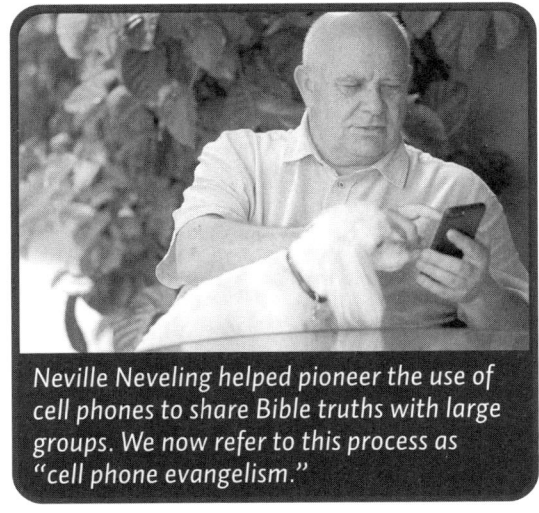

Neville Neveling helped pioneer the use of cell phones to share Bible truths with large groups. We now refer to this process as "cell phone evangelism."

The Dutch farmers in Namibia and South Africa are so spread out over vast territories that the best way to connect with them is through WhatsApp on their cell phones. Neville was sending out the Bible messages to more than 200 Dutch farming families, as well as anyone else who requested them.

Where had he gotten the material for these messages? That's where the story gets interesting.

The year before, Neville had wanted to organize a camp meeting for all the Dutch farmers in the area, and he'd invited Jonathan, an Adventist attorney from Southern California, to be the speaker.

Jonathan had gladly accepted. Then, a few months later, when I was asked to organize evangelistic meetings in Eastern Europe and needed volunteers to help, I also thought of Jonathan, whom I knew personally. He had agreed to help me coordinate the 17-night evangelistic meetings and find speakers for the event. That's when he thought of Neville, who had invited him to speak in Namibia just a few months before.

Neville agreed to go and had preached the *Revelation of Hope* series we provided. The meetings were a success. They were part of the AWR/Total Member Involvement initiative with more than 4,000 preaching sites throughout Eastern Europe.

Neville became so excited about the series that he decided to use it for evangelistic meetings with the Dutch Afrikaans-speaking community in Africa using his cell phone, which is what Antoinette had been listening to and studying.

When Neville completed his first evangelistic cell phone series using WhatsApp, God gave him an astounding 150 decisions for baptism—all from his cell phone witnessing!

I decided to ask Neville to work with us at AWR to help expand cell phone evangelism so even greater things could be accomplished by the power of the Holy Spirit. What started with what we thought were astounding results blew us away! Since teaming up with AWR, Neville has trained thousands of people on cell phone evangelism in some of the most unexpected places, including across Africa, Japan, the Philippines, India, Europe, South America and the United States! Since then, he's finished a series where more than 10,000 listened and shared sermons, and over 6,000 from around the world have requested baptism!

Isn't God amazing? He put all these pieces together and brought us full circle! I had asked God, "Why, why, why?" on that dark night on a bumpy road, and now we finally understood. Meeting Antoinette had been God-ordained. He used her to connect us with the one person in all of Africa who had come up with modern-day cell phone evangelism!

But what about Antoinette? The next year, we were back in Livingstone for a huge baptism—the one we had been planning the year before. A total of 17,969 people were baptized as a result of 1,075 AWR360° evangelistic meetings! And the best part? I had the privilege of baptizing Antoinette.

Duane McKey had the privilege of baptizing a joyful Antoinette in South Africa.

BARBIE'S INCREDIBLE STORY
The Miracle at Kashira Village

BARBIE AND HER HUSBAND DRIES LIVE IN KASHIRA Village, Namibia, near what is called the Caprivi Strip. They're both farmers and Afrikaners—descended from people who immigrated to South Africa in the 17th century from Holland.

The land where their farm is located belongs to the African people, and anyone who wants to work the land must obtain permission from the area chief. The arrangement is unique in that the land must be shared with the community, and major decisions are also communicated to the entire village.

Barbie and Dries had requested some of this land, and were perfectly happy with this arrangement, getting along very well with the local people. Their life would have continued uneventfully, except Barbie had a close friend named Elize, who just happened to be a Seventh-day Adventist.

When Elize's church decided to do the AWR cell phone evangelism series, she added Barbie to her WhatsApp group, so Barbie and her husband started receiving evangelistic sermons on their cell phones. Every night after their farm chores were done, they would listen to the presentations and then discuss what they had heard. When they heard the presentation on the Sabbath, they were immediately impressed that they should follow Jesus and keep the Sabbath.

Their conviction was so great that, in keeping with the local custom, the next morning they called the village people together and informed them that they would now be keeping God's Sabbath holy and would not worship on Sunday anymore. They explained to the villagers that the Bible was very clear on this.

The villagers listened intently to everything Barbie and Dries said, and in the end agreed that if that was what the Bible said, then they would keep the Sabbath too! So Barbie did the only thing she could think to do: she got the people together every Sabbath and played the AWR cell phone sermons for everyone to listen—all this before she and her husband had a chance to tell Elize that they wanted to be baptized!

When they listened to the presentation on health, they started a garden project where they not only produced healthy foods for themselves, but also for the communities around them. By now, they were getting together for prayer meeting, a weekly lesson study and Sabbath services—all the while, the group kept growing and growing.

Barbie (left) accepted Elize's invitation to receive an AWR evangelistic series via WhatsApp on her cell phone.

At the end of the cell phone series, Barbie and Dries were baptized—to the delight of Elize and her church!

But the story doesn't end there.

Soon, Barbie decided they must have a church. Dries and the villagers started working on the structure while Barbie and the ladies cleared the land. For starters, the church would have steel pillars and a corrugated tin roof. Barbie and some of the villagers worked on making bricks that would eventually be used to build the church walls. When we learned Barbie's story, AWR decided to help raise funds for the new church.

As if all this weren't exciting enough, while they were working on the church structure, they received a visit from the chief of another village. He told them the most amazing story: he had accepted the Sabbath truth many years before but had thought he was all alone in his decision. Ever since, he had been looking for others who believed as he did. Then one day, he'd heard about Barbie and Dries. He was so happy to hear there were others who believed as he did, so he decided to come and see for himself.

He said, "I have talked to my village and we, the whole village, want to join the Seventh-day Adventist Church! We all want to receive Bible studies."

The following Friday, the chief, along with 50 people from his village, walked the 40 miles to Kashira Village. The walk was through rough terrain, and it took them all day, but they arrived by nightfall and slept in makeshift shelters so they could worship together on Sabbath morning.

As I write this letter, the group that began with just Barbie and Dries—and grew to 52 people from their Kashira Village—has now grown to more than 200 people! Not long after, the first Seventh-day Adventist church that began solely from cell phone evangelism was dedicated in Kashira Village.

Barbie, here with Cami Oetman, had the joy of witnessing the birth of the very first Adventist church formed from cell phone evangelism.

No matter how small a part we may play—even using a simple cell phone—God can turn it into something spectacular.

MACHIEL VAN WYK, THE AFRIKANER FARMER
"When God Sent a Text Message..."

MACHIEL WAS FROM A DUTCH REFORMED BACKGROUND, but over time, he realized that some things he'd been taught were not correct, especially when he discovered that baptism was by immersion. So he left the Dutch Reformed Church and joined the Apostolic Faith Mission.

But after a while, he said something didn't feel right with his new church either. So he prayed to God and said, "Lord, please send someone my way who will guide me in the truth. I need the truth—nothing other than the truth."

Meet Machiel Van Wyk.

In that very moment, as he opened his eyes, he received a message on his phone through WhatsApp that said, "I would like to send you Bible studies."

Machiel didn't know the sender. He would later learn it had come from Neville Neveling, but the interesting thing is that neither man knows how this came about. Machiel says he never spoke to anybody nor asked anyone for Bible studies, and never gave his cell phone number to anyone. And to this day, Neville denies ever sending him that message, or even having his number. But the message was on Machiel's screen, and he immediately responded, "Yes." He had just prayed asking God to send someone, and he accepted it as God's answer.

Machiel joined the Bible studies, and very soon he was convinced he'd found the truth. He shared that when he first learned that the Sabbath was on Saturday and not on Sunday, he was very upset. "I grew up in the Dutch Reformed Church and they have a love of the Ten Commandments. I love them myself, too. They would read them every Sunday. I consider them the heartbeat of the Scriptures! So I was decimated when I found out that people have been lying to me and to the world for such a long time about something that is so important as the Sabbath. I immediately decided I would honor God's Sabbath on the right day."

There was something else that Machiel had wanted to know for a very long time. He wanted to understand the book of Revelation. "I desperately needed to understand that book, and no matter where I went, nobody could explain it to me. And then here, in this cell phone evangelism study, the book of Revelation was explained, and that has been an amazing experience for me."

Being an Afrikaner farmer in South Africa is dangerous. In recent years, many farmers have been killed by marauding rebel groups. When Machiel was asked if he was worried about security on his farm, he said, "Yes, it's bad. They have attacked farms all around us. But I've always lived my life in a very simple manner. God always comes first, and I don't do anything without first asking Him and letting God lead me." He then shared two incidents in which he saw God's hand intervene on his behalf.

THE BULLETS THAT DIDN'T FIRE

"Once a group of men came to the farm. They were shouting as they walked toward me. One of them had a gun that he pointed at me and started firing even as he walked and shouted. The bullets were flying out of the gun, but they were falling to the ground right in front of him. Not a single shot went off, and when the man had emptied the magazine and there were no bullets left, they all looked in astonishment at the gun that hadn't fired a single round."

Machiel said he picked up those bullets and put them in a gun that carried the same type of bullets, and every single one of them fired correctly when he pulled the trigger. He said, "I'm sure that God and His angels protected me, because I allow myself to be guided and directed by the Lord and only the Lord. I trust Him 100 percent and was probably not ready to die that day."

WHO PUT OUT THE FIRE?

Some time passed, and the men decided that if they could not shoot Machiel, they would set his farm on fire. "It was a windy day, and those Highveld red grasses burn so quickly that the flames can easily reach two stories high. When I looked out over the field and saw the fire, I looked up to the sky and said, "God, please, no animals and no humans. Please protect us and don't let any harm come to my family or my animals."

The flames were raging toward the cattle corral and the houses, and the wind was blowing. "I was trying my best, but there wasn't much I could do. The flames came right up to the fence of the cattle corral, and right there they stopped and the fire went out. The burn marks are still there, and if you look at the fence, the fire side is scorched black, but the other side is normal."

But that wasn't the end of the fires, because more fires were set that day and into the night, and Machiel struggled to put them out. By 2 a.m., he was too tired to continue, so he said, "Lord, I can't do it anymore. I'm tired and need to sleep. I leave it in your hands."

He went to bed and instantly fell asleep, but two hours later, he woke up and looked out. His neighbor's farm was burning, so Machiel phoned him and said, "Why haven't you called me to help you? Your field is burning!"

And the neighbor replied, "I didn't call because I figured you were busy. I saw the veld burning on your side, and saw you had your hands full with your helpers busy killing the flames and putting out fires."

In that moment, Machiel understood. "I realized the Lord had sent a team of angels, because I wasn't there. I was asleep, and I didn't have any helpers."

God had fought the fires for him, because he trusted his life and everything he had to Jesus.

Machiel's experience is especially moving because it confirms again that God has children all around the world who are waiting and ready to hear God's final call and respond. They will be among those who, when the time comes, will not bow down to Baal but will stand with God's people. By thousands of voices all over the earth, the final call will be given, and the earth will be brought to take a stand.

When reflecting on this story, Neville said, "Nobody gave me Machiel's name or cell phone number, so it must have been God who texted him."

Yes! And God calls each one of us, maybe not by cell phone, but with opportunities He places in our path—opportunities not only to know Him better, but to help others learn His wonderful truth.

21
THE MIRACLE OF THE TITHING COWS

With God, Nine-Tenths Is More Than Ten!

I GREW UP ON A REGISTERED JERSEY FARM IN central Oklahoma. Jersey cows are known for their pretty fawn color and beautiful brown eyes. They're also noted for producing the best milk with the most cream. My parents milked between 60-80 cows every day in an old-style stanchion barn.

Mother loved her cows and knew them each by name since she did most of the milking herself, spending 6-8 hours a day with them. Milking cows was quite an experience and backbreaking work. It required bending over repeatedly to wash and dry the cows' udders and put the milkers on. Then repeating the process over again whenever a cow kicked a milker off. Not surprisingly, my dad used to say, "Everything I have I owe to udders!"

For 50 years, my parents ran that dairy farm. Mom was 83 when they finally sold the cows. Through the years they had many cows, mostly Jerseys and a few black Angus. In the spring, when new baby calves were born, it was exciting to watch them grow from heifers into milk-producing cows, who in turn would produce more babies. But in all those years, I remember only one set of twin calves ever being born.

It is considered a rare event when a cow has more than one calf at a time—some would call it historic. So you can imagine my surprise when I heard the most amazing story from one of our AWR listeners in Tanzania—a native

Maasai who began giving his tithe with cows. What happened next astonished everyone around him and is nothing short of a miracle.

THE MAASAI CATTLE OWNER

When we were in Tanzania, we met Abraham, a wealthy Maasai cattle owner, who shared the following story. He had attended a series of evangelistic meetings and decided to be baptized. Despite his wealth, he had never learned to read or write, so when he discovered our AWR station in Tanzania, he was overjoyed and regularly listened to the programs on his radio.

As he listened, he learned many new things about being a faithful Adventist—from healthful living to returning an honest tithe. Owning more than 1,000 cows and large herds of sheep and goats scattered over Tanzania and Kenya, he decided that he would strive to be faithful with all his holdings. So he placed his cattle in large pens and counted them as they walked through a chute. He counted cows 1-9 as they went through, and number 10 he marked for God.

Abraham, a Maasai cattle owner, counted out and marked every tenth cow for God. And what happened next shocked everyone he knew!

This went on for a while to the amazement of his friends and all the people who knew him. You see, for a Maasai, cattle are almost more important than people. You just don't give them away! His friends watched him go through this process again and again, and they began to mock him, laughing and saying he was crazy.

But the laughter abruptly stopped some nine months later, when 40 of his cows gave birth to twins, and many goats and sheep had triplets! God was blessing him just as He had blessed Jacob—Abraham's grandson from the Bible—when the cattle changed colors with Laban's changing rules so that Jacob's herds were always blessed. It was God who blessed Jacob's cattle so they produced the right colors, and it was God who was now blessing this modern-day Abraham.

Abraham and all the Maasai who mocked him were learning that with God, nine-tenths goes much further than keeping all 10 for yourself!

Abraham was so happy at how God was blessing him that he decided to give double tithe. When counting his cattle, he began counting eight and giving two to God! And God blessed him even more.

I have seen many times how—to put it in farming terms—God's scoop shovel is bigger than ours. You simply can't outgive God!

But there's more, because God's blessings come with ripple effects.

In open ranges like in Kenya and Tanzania, thieves often come and steal cattle. But something interesting began to happen. Whenever any of Abraham's cows were stolen, they would always find their way back home, inevitably returning to Abraham's herds as if unseen hands were guiding them home. It got to the point where the thieves had become very nervous about stealing Abraham's livestock!

A few months later, the Tanzanian Union Mission President, Dr. Godwin Lekundayo, told me that many of those who had mocked and laughed at Abraham now wanted in on the same blessings he is receiving, so they approached our local pastors with a request.

"We want to tithe our cattle as well, just like Abraham is doing," they said.

"But you're not Adventist," our pastors replied in surprise.

"We don't care! We want God's blessings, so we want to pay tithe with our cows, goats and sheep too!" they insisted.

But there's more! In a village near where Abraham lives, a local chief built a pond, and during the dry season would charge other Maasai cattle owners to water their livestock there. One day, Abraham had an inspired idea. He decided to build a larger pond and let the cattle owners water their cattle there for free, but on one condition. He hired a Bible worker to preach to them about Jesus while they were watering their animals! The cattle owners were so grateful for the free water that they gladly listened to the message!

People have been so impressed by Abraham's ongoing testimony and generous spirit that many have expressed a desire to belong to Abraham's church. This is very significant, as the Maasai are traditionally difficult to convert to Christianity.

Duane and Abraham stand together in front of Abraham's cattle.

But Abraham's testimony is more powerful than tradition, and many Maasai also listen to Adventist World Radio. They have been surprised to learn that we have some beliefs in common with them. Traditionally, the Maasai believe in God and not in ancestral worship or witchcraft. They also believe that when you die, you are asleep. This has helped to open their hearts and minds to receive the full gospel message.

So far, thanks to Abraham's testimony, 70 Maasai have accepted Jesus and been baptized. And they all listen to Adventist World Radio!

When we installed the radio station in Tanzania targeting the many Maasai tribes, we never dreamed of the impact it would have on Abraham. We didn't even know Abraham. But God knew him, and He knew this sincere man was waiting with a ready heart to listen and receive the full gospel message.

YOUNG-WOONG'S TESTIMONY
"It Was the First Time I Had Seen a Bible"

WE RECEIVE MANY LETTERS AND PRAYER REQUESTS at Adventist World Radio, and we pray over them every week during our staff worship meetings. Here is one letter that touched our hearts:

"Since I was a child, I was taught that religion was the opiate of the masses, so I had no interest in religion and had no concept of God. In school I learned that Jesus was just a fictional character created in history books.

When I graduated from college, I went to Beijing, China, to become a civil servant. I didn't lack anything and was happy. But one day, while working in my office, I received a letter from South Korea. It was from Adventist World Radio. It contained Christian material, and I assumed they had sent me the letter in error.

After a couple days of deliberation as to whether or not to respond, I wrote them a letter. My intention was to say I was not a Christian and not interested, but instead, I ended up awkwardly requesting a Bible! This was not the desire of my heart, but something strange compelled me to ask. I didn't think they would go to the trouble of sending it, so I forgot about it.

To my surprise, soon after, I received a package in my office. It contained a Bible and Bible studies. It was the first time in my life that I had seen a Bible. I read the first page, but the story sounded too long and foolish, so I snapped the Bible shut. Instead, I flipped through the lessons, but what caught my interest was the health study that was included. It said that if I answered the questions correctly, I would receive a prize—so I did.

When the next package arrived, they suggested that I listen to AWR's Korean broadcast in China. Since it was in my mother tongue, it piqued my curiosity. Besides, when I got home at night, I was bored with nothing to do, so instead, I began listening to the broadcast. Soon it became the most exciting part of my day. I even changed my lifestyle in order to wake up earlier to listen to the 6 a.m. broadcast as well. I enjoyed it so much that I felt it was like an addictive soap opera!

As I listened to the Bible teachings, I became convicted they were the Word of God, and the conviction began growing in me that I must make a decision. I spent many sleepless nights struggling but knowing I must follow Jesus.

In the end, I surrendered the communist government position I held and went to South Korea to study at Sahmyook Adventist University to become a pastor. Today, I am a pastor in China. When I look back on my life, I see God directing me every step of the way."

What a powerful testimony! God has a plan, and you and I have been called to help share the gospel message around the world.

Something that Young-Woong said has really stayed with me:

"It may be that in Christian countries, and even in South Korea, the messages of AWR are not as appreciated as they are in places where God's Word is not permitted, but in China and North Korea, these programs are vital. Even in places where the reception is weak, people are willing to listen for hours at a time.

AWR introduced not only me, but my whole family, to Christ. That's why whenever I visit South Korea, I always pay my respects by visiting the AWR studio. This is the place that birthed my new soul, my new hometown. My one hope is for AWR to reach the corners of North Korea and draw out people like me into the light of Jesus.

Thank you, AWR, for your efforts. You changed my life."

23

MIRACLE IN UKRAINE
God Used a Cat

WE HAVE SO MANY STORIES FROM SO MANY different countries that sometimes it's hard to decide which ones to share. But there is one story we can't leave out, and it's from Ukraine. You may have heard many distressing reports depicting the horrors of war, but even in the midst of disaster, God is still there, working to save the lost—and He doesn't forget His children.

Back in 2022, Adventist World Radio purchased a semi-trailer truck to be used as a movable radio station and medical clinic throughout Ukraine. It has been a blessing, even today, as we park it in different parts of the country, in front of Adventist churches, and offer medical checkups and share solar-powered Godpods.

You may have heard of the massacre in the city of Bucha in 2022, one of the hardest-hit cities that showed the depths of human depravity when Russian troops razed the city as they advanced toward Kyiv. They were eventually repelled, but not before leaving behind destruction and devastation. When our AWR truck arrived in the city after the destruction, we learned firsthand from the local church leaders what had happened.

You may not know this, but in Bucha we have a thriving Adventist college. When word spread that the Russians were approaching, and details of the atrocities committed in the nearby city of Irpin became known, the people started to flee. Many were unable to do so in time, so where did they seek refuge? In our Adventist college! They knew we were Christians and felt it was their only hope.

Most of our students had evacuated in time and only a handful remained, including a few faculty members and a pastor. The people hid in several of the school basements, and at first they would gather for meetings in the chapel, but a mortar shell landed right outside the building and all the windows shattered. After that, they didn't take chances and moved everyone to the basements.

For two weeks, they remained hidden, cooking food in the cafeteria and bringing it down to the shelters. The pastor ministered to the people, preaching sermons and putting up a sheet for his projector. All during this time, they could hear bombs falling and mortar shells landing nearby. But not a single building from our school was destroyed. Everyone was praying, asking God for protection and guidance. Most had family in other places, and their plan was to make an escape as soon as they could.

They all finally decided to leave on a particular date and made preparations. But that night, the pastor had a dream, and in his dream, he saw terrible things taking place when they left: people being shot and tortured, and children killed. He woke up in a cold sweat and felt the dream had been from God. So he communicated this to the group and they agreed to wait. Later that day, they received word that a group of civilians had been killed trying to escape that morning.

GOD SENDS A CAT

The group continued to pray, specifically asking God to show them when they should leave. Now, one thing to note is that when all the people fled to our school, they brought a few things with them—including their pets! They couldn't bear to leave them behind and kept them warm under blankets or

Many of those who took refuge in the school also brought their beloved pets with them.

inside cozy bags. The animals seemed to sense the danger and their behavior was exemplary.

But on one occasion, when a bomb fell nearby, it spooked one of the cats, and he bolted out of the basement and disappeared. The children of that family were heartbroken. The pets were a great comfort not only to them, but to everyone, and now their cat was gone.

Somehow, the group made the decision that they would ask God for a sign as to when they should leave, and they decided that when the cat returned, it would be their sign. Lo and behold, a few days later, to everyone's joy, the cat returned, and they took this as the sign. The pastor also felt that God was telling them to leave.

They divided into two groups, with the women and children leaving in vehicles, and the men on foot. The scenes they encountered along the way were of devastation all around: giant blown-out craters on the road, cars and tanks burned to a crisp, corpses strewn on the frozen ground. The vehicles made slow progress as they carefully navigated the road. Suddenly, coming toward them, they saw a Russian tank.

Everyone froze and the children began to scream in terror. But right before the tank reached them, it abruptly turned down a side road. As incredible as it may seem, the leader from the school riding with them had the impression that they should follow the tank. It made no sense, but that's what they did, following at a distance. The tank took them through several obstacles, and pretty soon the group realized it was leading them directly to a safe zone! They later learned if they had continued on the road they were on, they would all have been killed.

All of them—including the men on foot—made it out of the war zone and to safety.

Later, when several recounted their long ordeal in hiding, they said it was a terrifying time, but they felt peace whenever the pastor shared the Word of God with them.

AN ATHEIST IN THE GROUP

One of the people who sought shelter in our school was an avowed atheist. She was disabled and couldn't walk. Her friends carried her to the shelter. For two weeks, she listened to the pastor's sermons and the prayers ascending daily to God's throne. At first she was annoyed, but God was working in her heart. She was a witness to answered prayer and was in one of the cars when they were delivered from an impossible situation. But above all, she witnessed the love of the group of Adventist believers as they ministered to each other.

When they all made it to safety, they took this lady to a care home for people with disabilities. That first night alone, for the first time in her life, she prayed: "God, I've never believed in You before, but if You hear me, please help me to walk again."

The next morning, she got out of bed—and was able to walk! Her family was called to come for her. They were not in the area, and when they heard this, they couldn't believe it. She hadn't walked in years. But when they learned she now believed in God, they were convinced and said: "We believe her change of heart is a much bigger miracle than the healing of her legs!"

THE BLUEBERRY FARMER AND THE METHODIST CHURCH
The Sunday-to-Sabbath Church?

A BLUEBERRY FARMER IN TROUT CREEK, MONTANA, was chatting with some of his customers, when they mentioned their local Methodist church needed a pastor. The farmer—who happened to be Adventist—said, "We just got a new pastor, and he's free on Sundays."

Pretty soon Pastor Donavon Kack got a call from one of the elders at the Methodist church: "Can you preach for us on Sundays?"

Pastor Kack replied, "Sure, I'll be happy to. But do you have any restrictions?"

A conversation with a blueberry farmer led to a miraculous chain of events.

The elder said, "As long as you preach the Bible, we're fine with that. You can preach whatever you want."

So Pastor Kack began preaching at the Methodist church every Sunday. A few months into this routine, the members asked Pastor Kack, "Why aren't we growing? We want to grow." There were about 8-10 members attending at any given time in that beautiful church.

I should point out that Pastor Kack had been an evangelist for many years, and had only returned to pastoral duties when he learned that his conference president shared his vision of what pastoral work should be: evangelism and church planting, while relying on the members to run the church. So let's just say he knew a little about church growth.

"You want to grow?" Pastor Kack asked them. "I know how to do that. First, fervently pursue a relationship with Jesus. And second, get back to the Bible."

This resonated with the Methodist group, so they put up a banner outside their church that said, "Back to the Bible With Pastor Donavon Kack!"

A month later, they came to him again and said, "We know you used to be an evangelist. Would you consider doing a prophecy series for us?"

Pastor Kack replied, "Yes, but it's impossible to teach Revelation without getting into the Sabbath issue. The only way to preach about prophecy is to be honest about the Sabbath."

They said, "Hey, if it's in the Bible, we want it!"

So, they began the meetings and invited their community. And you know what? They never went back to Sunday worship again! The meetings ran several nights a week, including Sunday night. They substituted that for their regular Sunday service. Four nights after the Sabbath subject was presented, they came to Pastor Kack and said, "We have decided we want to be Seventh-day Methodists!"

But by the time the evangelistic series was over, the church had decided they wanted to become Seventh-day Adventists.

Pastor Kack shared what he did next:

> "Suddenly, I had a brand-new Adventist congregation! They were young in the faith, and I wanted to give them a bigger picture of our work and worldwide mission, so I began searching for videos to share with them. I had worked with Pastor McKey years before and knew of his mission work, so I went to the

AWR website. That's when I discovered the AWR mission story videos with Cami Oetman. I began showing one every Sabbath and the people absolutely loved them. As a result, every month they are giving to AWR. Thank you for what you are doing. Today, this is a very vibrant, enthusiastic and growing church!"

Several Adventists from the surrounding area decided to join this new congregation and help out. The group is now renting the Methodist building and raising funds to build their own church.

Isn't that amazing? A Sunday-to-Sabbath church right here in America! We love stories like this that show what God can do when we are willing to step out in faith, unafraid to present the whole message. When we remember we are not working alone and that God's Spirit is the one convicting hearts, we will not be afraid to present the whole truth.

This Methodist (now Adventist) congregation gathers each Sabbath in Trout Creek, Montana.

THE 51-YEAR DREAM
"Before You Were Born, I Knew You..."

MY WIFE KATHY AND I MET DARYL AND MARY JO several years ago at a church potluck. As we talked, they expressed some genuine concerns about problems in the church. We could have talked problems all day—because they do exist—but instead, I encouraged them to join us on a mission trip, something they had never considered doing.

That night, they called us to say they had been unable to stop thinking about our offer, and felt God wanted them to go to Africa.

After making some arrangements with their medical business, they joined us on a mission trip to Kenya. Daryl preached a full evangelistic series and Mary Jo gave the health talks every evening.

Later, Daryl told me that as he preached, he was transformed. Many things that he had not really believed or understood about our prophetic message, he suddenly grasped as he shared it with others. He became very excited about the Adventist message and fell in love with Jesus all over again.

Daryl and Mary Jo had a medical business, which hadn't been doing well, but suddenly it began to flourish. So they made several more trips to Africa, each time with new projects in mind: a water purification system for the people near Lake Victoria, a feeding program for orphans whose parents had died of AIDS, and an irrigation system with solar energy for growing vegetables for the orphanage.

GOD KNOWS IT ALL

Over the years I received great reports from them about the work they were doing and how blessed they felt at the opportunity to help others and share the gospel message. Then Daryl shared with me an experience that shook him to the core.

He was back in Kenya preaching another evangelistic series in a mountain town.

He had cleared the hillside and set up loudspeakers so the villagers could hear even if they couldn't go to the meeting site. The meetings were progressing well, with a large crowd in attendance. Then a week into the presentations, when Daryl spoke about baptism, an older lady approached him after the meeting and said, "I want to be baptized."

This was surprising, as in Daryl's experience, older people were generally more set in their ways and had a harder time comprehending and accepting new truth, but then Esther (that was her name) told Daryl the most amazing story.

"I remember a dream I had 51 years ago . . ." she began.

Esther heard Daryl's voice in a dream 51 years earlier!

Daryl's ears pricked up because he was 51 years old himself. The lady continued, "I was asleep and dreamed that I heard an American's voice that echoed all around the mountain behind my house. God told me in the dream that when I heard that voice, I would know it was the truth."

She went on, "The first time I heard you speak, and heard your voice echo around the mountain, I knew it was the voice I'd heard 51 years ago. So I know this is the truth, and I want to be baptized."

Daryl was moved to tears and so excited as he recounted the story to me. He said, "To think that God knew me and knew of this moment even when I was first born 51 years ago!"

I was moved, too. I realized that God had orchestrated our encounter with Daryl and Mary Jo at that potluck all those years ago. God knew Kathy and I would encourage this dear couple to venture into mission work. He knew how they would be able to help the orphans with food and pure water. He knew of the solar-powered irrigation system that would help the orphanage grow their own vegetables. And He knew many people would be led to Christ through their ministry. God knew it all!

God knew Daryl before he was born, just like He knows you and me. He says, "Before I formed you in the womb I knew you, before you were born, I set you apart . . ." (Jeremiah 1:5)

God knows your name, and "even the very hairs on your head are numbered." He knows the desires of your heart and hears you when you call. And He invites you and me to be His light to the world. Talk about an amazing job offer!

If I've learned anything during the last 50+ years in ministry, it's that when you give your life to Him and accept His call to service, hang on, because you'll be in for the ride of your life! I know I was.

I could never have imagined for myself the life of faith and adventure that God had in store for me. I know He can do the same for you. So if you haven't asked Him yet, I challenge you to give God a chance and see what He will do.

"There are possibilities for work to be done by you for Jesus that you have never dreamed of." (*Sons and Daughters of God,* p. 272)